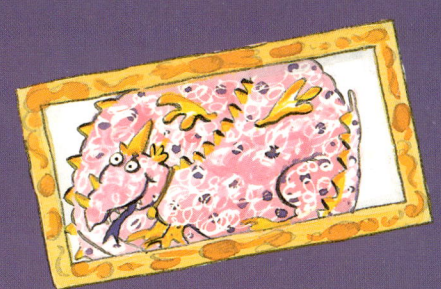

Tiny the Troll's Friendly Monster Stories

ORCHARD BOOKS
96 Leonard Street, London EC2A 4RH
Orchard Books Australia
14 Mars Road, Lane Cove, NSW 2066
First published in Great Britain in 1995
Illustrations © Sonia Holleyman 1995
The right of Sonia Holleyman has been asserted by her
in accordance with the Copyright, Designs and Patents Act, 1988.
A CIP catalogue record for this book is available from the British Library.
1 85213 945 5
Printed in Belgium

Tiny the Troll's Friendly Monster Stories

Sonia Holleyman
Compiled by Penny Worms

ORCHARD BOOKS

GRANNY MONSTER'S BED-TIME STORY

Andrew Matthews

If you are a naughty little monster, listen to this story very carefully....

While the Monster and Mrs Monster were out at the Tip-Top Monster Do, Granny Monster took care of Baby. Baby Monster was happy. She made her rubber duck go 'BAMP!' in the bath, and when she was clean and dry, Granny gave her a slice of porcupine flan and a mug of rhinoceros milk. When Baby had finished the last drop of milk, Granny looked at her sternly.

"Time for baby monsters to be in bed!" she said.

Baby Monster stuck out her bottom lip. She didn't feel sleepy. "Me a story, Granny!" she pleaded.

"Very well, I'll tell you a story," Granny agreed. "But you must get into bed and snuggle down first."

Baby Monster jumped into bed and snuggled down so far that only her eyes and the tip of her snout showed over the blankets.

"Long, long ago," began Granny, "there lived a beautiful baby monster, just like you. But though she was beautiful, she was naughty! She wouldn't eat her dinner, she wouldn't have a bath and she wouldn't go to bed when she was told."

"Ooh!" said Baby Monster.

"Everybody told her that something awful would happen to her if she wasn't good," went on Granny, "but she wouldn't listen. She carried on being wicked!"

"Well, one morning she woke up and found that something awful had happened to her. She had changed!"

"Coo!" said Baby Monster.

"She jumped out of bed and ran to the mirror to look at herself," said Granny, "and she saw something horrible! Instead of having pink and orange fur, she had long golden hair! Her scales and feathers were gone! She had soft skin! Her claws and hooves had turned into hands and feet! She had two blue eyes and a small

straight nose!"

"Woo!" gasped Baby Monster.

"Her lips were red," said Granny, "and her nice sharp monster fangs had turned into little teeth as white as snow. And the strangest thing of all was... SHE ONLY HAD ONE BOTTOM!"

"Hoo!" shivered Baby Monster.

"Well," said Granny, "when her mum monster and dad monster saw her, you could have knocked them down with a dandelion! They didn't know what to do! She couldn't fly, she couldn't knock down trees, she was useless! The only thing she could do was cook, but what she cooked was so horrid, she was the only one who could eat it! Do you know what kind of things she used to cook?"

"Noo!" said Baby Monster.

"Fish fingers and chips!" said Granny. "Spaghetti rings on toast!"

"YEE-UK!" squealed Baby Monster.

"It was then that Mum Monster and Dad Monster knew what had happened to their naughty daughter," said Granny sadly. "She had turned into a person! She had to be sent far away, to the place where people live, and eat hamburgers and wear skirts and trousers!"

"Ugh!" cried Baby Monster.

"So," warned Granny, "if you're naughty and don't do as you're told, you might turn into a person too!"

"Me good!" whispered Baby Monster with wide eyes.

"Yes!" smiled Granny. "You're very good! Now go to sleep and have lovely monstrous dreams!"

And Baby Monster did.

I was visiting my Aunt Magnolia on the Isles of Magic when I met the most charming dragon. He showed me a photograph of his family....

THE DRAGON OF AN ORDINARY FAMILY

Margaret Mahy

There was this family called Belsaki. Mr Belsaki, Mrs Belsaki, and their little boy, Gaylord Belsaki. They were quite ordinary people, their house was a quite ordinary house in a quite ordinary street – and no doubt they would have lived quite ordinary lives for ever, if one morning Mrs Belsaki hadn't called Mr Belsaki a FUDDY-DUDDY. It was like this.

The day began with breakfast, as usual, with Mr Belsaki rushing through his hot oatmeal, a little late for work, as usual. Just as he was rushing out of the door, hat and briefcase in hand, Mrs Belsaki called after him, "On your way home, dear, stop in at the pet shop and buy Gaylord a pet."

"A pet!" exclaimed Mr Belsaki. "What does he want a pet for? We haven't got room anyway."

"Nonsense!" said Mrs Belsaki. "Of course he can have a pet. And we have room for an ELEPHANT, if Gaylord wanted one."

"An ELEPHANT!" Mr Belsaki turned slightly pale and his mouth hung open in a foolish fashion.

"All right, all right," Mrs Belsaki said impatiently, "he doesn't want an elephant, as it happens. He just wants a puppy – or perhaps a little kitten. . . Don't be a FUDDY-DUDDY, Mr Belsaki!"

Mr Belsaki stamped out crossly, pulling his hat down over his ears, muttering, "Fuddy-duddy, fuddy-duddy, indeed!"

On his way home from work, Mr Belsaki went into the pet shop and looked around. He saw white mice and hamsters, puppies and kittens, all shades and kinds of birds, some sad-eyed goldfish, and a parrot called Joe, with a sign over him saying NOT FOR SALE.

Mr Belsaki glowered at them all and glared around the shop.

Then his eye caught a sign which said UNUSUAL PET, VERY CHEAP. In smaller lettering underneath, it said DRAGON, HOUSETRAINED, 50 cents.

"That is very reasonable," said Mr Belsaki to the pet shop man. "I suppose it isn't a very good breed of dragon."

The pet shop man sighed. "No, it's a good breed – the only breed," he explained. "But it's a very small one. . . And, too, there isn't much demand, you know."

Mr Belsaki hesitated, and the dragon blinked its violet-blue eyes at him and flicked his tongue out.

"I'll take it!" said Mr Belsaki loudly.

And that was how it happened that he came home with a tiny dragon in a shoebox.

"What on earth is in there?" Mrs Belsaki asked, surprised at the noisy snuffles from the shoebox.

"A dragon," replied Mr Belsaki triumphantly.

"A dragon!" Mrs Belsaki screamed.

"A DRAGON!" cried Gaylord in delight.

"It was cheap," Mr Belsaki answered, clutching the shoebox to him as if he was afraid that Mrs Belsaki might snatch it away. "You said I was a FUDDY-DUDDY," he added firmly, "and I am no such thing."

"You could have chosen something pretty," Mrs Belsaki complained. "A ginger kitten perhaps, or a budgie-bird that talks. . . And where will we keep a dragon?"

"We have room enough here to keep an ELEPHANT," Mr Belsaki reminded her.

So they kept the dragon, and it grew and grew.

It was a wonderful pet for Gaylord. He kept it in the shoebox for a while, then in a bird cage, then in a dog kennel. He painted a washtub for its food, with the word DRAGON on it in red.

The dragon grew and grew. Mrs Belsaki became quite proud of it. "It certainly gives a different look to the place," she remarked at least once a day. "It makes us a bit out of the ordinary."

Her friends said, "What on earth did you get that for?" But Mrs Belsaki always replied, "Mr Belsaki's a man with ideas, that's why!" And she always added, "He's not a FUDDY-DUDDY – not like some."

The dragon grew and grew.

Finally it filled almost the whole yard. It got so it could breathe out smoke and fire.

It even got big enough for Gaylord to ride.

Then it even got as big as an elephant. None of Mrs Belsaki's friends came to visit any more. They were rather afraid.

The dragon grew...

It grew bigger than an elephant!

It grew TOO big!

One day the Mayor came to look at the Belsakis' dragon. He studied it and studied it.

"It is much too big to keep in a built-up area," he said crossly. "Mr Belsaki, you are just an ordinary family, and you should stick to ordinary pets. Mr Belsaki, you must sell it. . . to a zoo. Or to a circus. . . or maybe to a handbag factory. Some people would pay a lot for dragon-skin."

Mr and Mrs Belsaki looked very worried and sad. They loved their dragon, but, beyond all doubt, it was growing too big. Besides, it cost so much to feed.

"We can't even afford to buy a Christmas tree, or go for a vacation this year," Mr Belsaki said gloomily.

"Well, I would rather have our dragon!" Gaylord cried.

"Well, you can't," the Mayor answered snappishly. "It is just too much! You have exactly one week to get rid of it."

And he marched away.

"As if we would sell our dragon!" Mrs Belsaki said indignantly. "And we certainly don't want him made into a handbag! Oh, if only we knew of a dragon-loving farmer. We would give him away to a really good farmer."

Then, for the first time, the dragon spoke. "As a matter of fact, it is getting a little cramped here for me, and I feel that, though I am fond of you all, I should shift to another place. . . How would you like to come with me for the Christmas holidays?"

"Where were you thinking of going?" Mr Belsaki asked.

"To the Isles of Magic," the dragon answered. "All dragons know the way there."

Mrs Belsaki thought for a moment. "Well, it could be all right. I'll go and pack."

So the Mayor, and Mrs Belsaki's friends, and their ordinary neighbours were amazed to see Mr and Mrs Belsaki and Gaylord Belsaki fly away on the dragon's back, that very day – off for their holidays – with their suitcases and shopping bags and baskets and paper boxes tied to the dragon's tail.

Higher and higher the dragon flew, way up into the clouds, and then, after a long time, he dropped down, down, down. There below them lay the bluest-blue sea, with the Isles of Magic spread across it, all gold and green as if summer leaves had been blown there by a dreaming wind.

Oh, the Isles of Magic! What would the Belsakis do on the Isles of Magic?

For the Isles of Magic, the dragon explained to them as they flew along, are the homes of all the wonderful, strange, fairy-tale people. What would an ordinary family with an ordinary home, with dustbins, a teapot and a neat, mowed lawn – what would they do on the Isles of Magic?

This is what the Belsakis did.

They walked in the forests, the green and gold, the dark and old forests. They saw the starry towers of castles rising above the trees, and princesses sitting in the windows, combing their hair, waiting for princes to come and rescue them. They met all manner of youngest sons – the youngest sons of kings, of millers, of cobblers and beggars – all seeking fortunes.

Some days they went sailing in a great galleon over shining seas, diving for pearls through deep, green water. They hunted and sailed with pirates, and buried treasure in golden sand on islands where parrots screamed and monkeys mocked in the palm trees. And all the while the Belsakis could hear mermaids singing among the great black rocks under the lacy veil of the spray.

On other days they searched for lost cities of ivory, cities of gold, forgotten and terribly old. Or they watched witches twitch their broomsticks over the sky.

On the far horizon, like mountains, giants moved on their mysterious business. From the windows of the castle they lived in, the Belsaki family watched them curiously and nervously.

When Christmas came they sang their carols around a tree covered in small candles, accommodatingly formed by hundreds of glow-worms – so high that a real star shivered, fragile and far, on its top.

Mr Belsaki's best present was a remarkable hubble-bubble hookah that played wild music while he smoked. Mrs Belsaki got a sewing basket set with emeralds, and with an ivory thimble and little silver scissors shaped like a stork. Gaylord got a chess set where little knights and queens and pawns came alive and chased one another all over the board.

At last the time came for them to go back home. The dragon stayed, for the Isles of Magic are the proper place for dragons.

Then the Belsaki family sailed off home on a flying carpet, and as a farewell present, the dragon gave Gaylord a tiny black kitten with an over-sized purr.

"Now," said Mrs. Belaski, her unpacking nearly done, as she looked lovingly around her kitchen, "we can settle down to be nice, ordinary people again. I'm very glad Mr Belaski is not a FUDDY-DUDDY, and I was fond of that dragon – but I must say it will be pleasant to relax with our neighbours again."

"Next Christmas," Gaylord asked hopefully, "can we visit the Isles of Magic and see our dragon again?"

"Who knows," said Mr Belsaki, a little wistfully, "we may never see him again. . ." Then he said, a little sadly, "I suppose we'll have to settle down and be an ordinary family. Perhaps no other magic will ever happen to us again."

Just then the little black kitten woke and sat up tall in Gaylord's lap. "I wouldn't be too sure of that," he murmured, and went back to sleep.

Once upon a time in the middle of a dark forest in a damp gloomy cave, there lived a hairy monster. He was the ugliest brute you had ever seen. He had an enormous head directly attached to two ridiculously tiny feet, so tiny that he could not run: he could not leave his cave.

The monster had a huge mouth, and two wet little green eyes, and out of his ears came two long thin arms which he used to catch mice.

The ugliest thing about the monster was that he had hair all over his body – on his nose, his feet, his back, his teeth, his eyes and everywhere else besides.

All this monster did was dream about eating people. Every day he sat at the entrance to his cave and said to himself again and again:

"I will definitely eat the very first person I meet."

But nobody ever passed the cave because the forest was so deep. And he never caught anyone because he could not run on his tiny feet. But still he sat, waiting patiently, repeating to himself:

"I will definitely eat the very first person I meet."

One day, while hunting in the forest, a king got lost among the trees. He was very close to the hairy monster's cave.

Suddenly two long thin arms shot out of the dark cave and caught the king.

"Ha, ha!" cried the evil beast, "at last I have something to eat that's more filling than a mouse."

And the monster opened his huge mouth.

"Wait, wait," cried the king, "I know something that is much tastier than me."

"And what's that?" demanded the monster.

"Little children are much more tender," said the king.

"Are they?" said the monster.

So the monster agreed to let the king go, so long as he came back with a child for him to eat, and he tied a thick rope to the king's leg to make sure that he did.

"Be warned," added the hairy monster, "if you try to trick me, I will pull the rope and you will be back here before you can say 'Hairy Monster'. Understand?"

"I understand," said the king.

The king mounted his horse and galloped off. At the edge of the forest he stopped, pulled out a large pair of scissors from his saddlebag and tried to cut the rope that attached him to the monster. But he couldn't.

"Ha ha," crowed the monster from far away. "You can't trick me."

Terribly unhappy, the king set off again. Soon he came to a village. Surely he would find a little child here. But to his disappointment the whole place was deserted, all the children were at school.

So the king galloped on with the rope still attached to his leg.

Eventually he saw his own castle in the distance and nearby a little girl running down the middle of the road.

"Ah!" he said to himself.

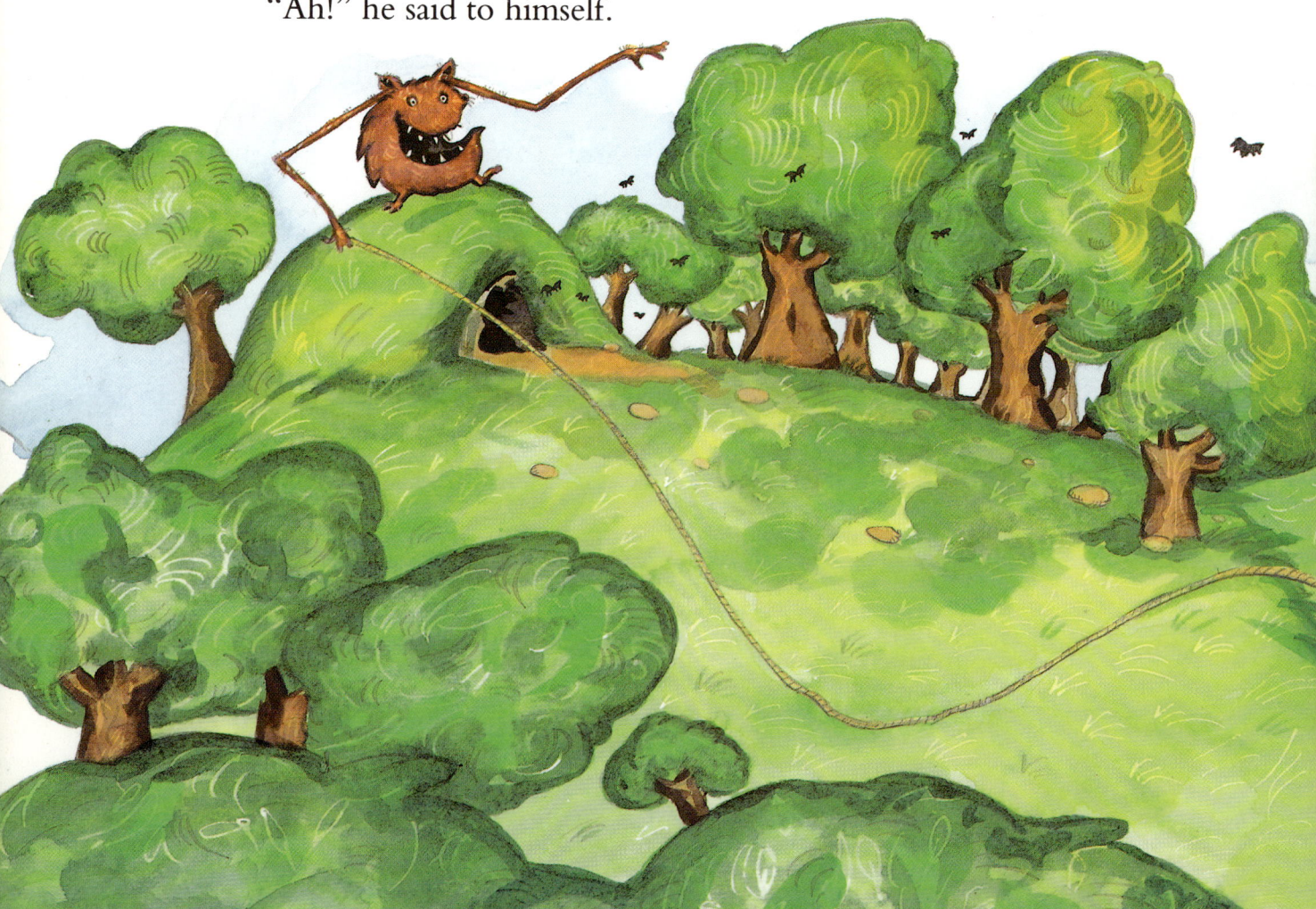

But imagine his horror when he realised that the little girl was none other than his very own daughter, little Lucy, who had sneaked out of the castle to buy some chocolate.

Furious in his desperation, the king roared at her:

"How many times have I told you that you are not allowed to eat chocolate before lunch, and I've told you never to leave the castle without permission!" He explained about the promise he had made to the monster.

At the other end of the rope, the hairy monster had heard every word.

"Ha ha," he sneered. "Don't you try and cheat me. I want that little girl and I want her now and if I don't get her. . ."

The king began to cry and little Lucy tried to comfort him. "Don't cry, Daddy," she said. "I don't mind going to the monster to get myself eaten."

"Oh, how wretched I feel!" sobbed the king. And he sat the little girl on his horse and returned to the monster's cave.

When they arrived the king dismounted. Trembling, he lifted his lovely little daughter off the horse. The monster untied the rope and ordered the king to leave at once.

Then the monster turned to Lucy who was waiting politely.

"You don't look very bothered," said the monster. "What a cheek!"

"Hairy beak," said Lucy innocently.

Taken by surprise, the monster found himself thinking that he probably did have a hairy beak since he had hair everywhere.

But this was no time for thinking. He had a meal to eat.

He groaned at the child: "I'll quickly make you feel more glum. . ."

"Hairy tum," trilled Lucy.

"Aaargh!" screeched the monster. "For that I am going to eat you, my little Lucy."

"Hairy toothy," said Lucy.

"What?" said the monster.

"I said hairy toothy, because you've got hair on your teeth," said little Lucy. (This was absolutely true. The monster did have hair on his teeth, just as he did on every other part of his body.)

"Keep quiet or you'll regret it!"

"Hairy feet."

"You are not being wise."

"Hairy eyes."

"All right. I am starting to count: one. . ."

"Hairy thumb."

". . . two. . ."

"Hairy view."

". . . three. . . and. . ."

"Hairy hand."

". . . four!"

"Hairy paw."

The monster threw himself on the ground in fury.

Then he shrieked: "Princesses should not be so rude – you weren't born in a slum!"

"Hairy bum."

"Right, we are through."

"Hairy poo."

This was too much for the monster. In his rage he started to swell. He swelled and swelled and swelled. . . until eventually he exploded into a thousand tiny pieces, every one of which turned into a beautifully coloured butterfly or sweet-smelling flower.

And from under the skin of the evil hairy monster appeared the sweetest, handsomest little boy you've ever seen.

"I am Prince Charming," he said with a beautiful smile. "You freed me from a horrible spell. I have been kept a prisoner for many years. Thank you, thank you. I would like you to marry me because I know we will be happy for ever."

Not surprisingly the little princess found the proposal irresistible. She accepted immediately and the two children flew away on the back of a giant butterfly.

And do you know from that day to this no one ever heard them talk of the hairy monster again.

Are you sitting comfortably? Then I'll begin.

At first nobody knew what the green grobblop was or even where it came from. Ben found it on the doorstep one Monday morning. He came running in from the garden calling to his mother.

"Come and see! There's a funny green hairy thing out here. It's ever so small and ever so sad. Can I play with it?"

Ben's mum, who was in the kitchen doing the washing, came to have a look.

"I don't know what it is," she said, "and it doesn't look very clean. I think I'd better give it a good wash before you play with it."

She always washed everything on a Monday. So she washed it. She was going to peg it up to dry when she heard it say, "Don't peg me upon the clothes line. A green grobblop like me should be put in a nice warm room."

Ben's mum was so surprised, she said, "Oh, I'm sorry!" and asked, "What did you say your name was?"

"I'm a green grobblop," it said, and it did look so small and sad. Ben's mum was a kind lady. She took it at once and put it on the curly, cuddly rug in the sitting room.

"That's much better," said the grobblop, nodding its small green head. "Now I should like tea and chocolate biscuits and some bananas."

"There is only one banana," said Ben, who was looking forward to eating it for his tea.

"Well, that will have to do for now then," sighed the grobblop, looking smaller and sadder than ever. "But in future, I would like three for my tea."

After he had eaten the banana, the grobblop had four helpings of biscuits. He was just drinking his fifth cup of tea when Ben's dad came home from work.

"What's that?" asked Ben's dad. When Ben and his mum told him, Ben's dad had to agree that the grobblop did look small and sad.

"And it will need to be well looked after," he said.

All the rest of the week the grobblop sat on the curly, cuddly rug. Ben's mum fed him and Ben played with him whenever he wanted. At the end of the week Ben's mum said: "I'm afraid I shall need some more money now that we have a grobblop to feed. It does eat rather a lot."

"I can see that," said Ben's dad, and he looked worried. He wasn't at all sure that his boss would pay him more money just because he now had a green grobblop to feed.

"Perhaps," he said, "when the green grobblop gets bigger and stronger, he'll be able to do some useful jobs about the house."

"I hope so," agreed Ben's mum. She had been doing everything for the grobblop, giving him the biggest helpings, letting him have the most comfortable place to sit in the sitting room and the warmest blankets on his bed.

"I can think of lots of useful things he could do," said Ben's mum.

No sooner was this said than the grobblop said, "I'll have to go to bed. I'm not at all well."

The doctor was called and he came almost at once. He wasn't used to treating grobblops, but he said, "He does look green and small and sad! He needs someone to look after him. He's to stay in bed a day or two and take this medicine to make him well and strong."

The grobblop liked his medicine almost as much as he liked tea and biscuits and bananas. He liked staying in bed even better than he liked lying on the curly, cuddly rug in the sitting room. So he stayed in bed and had all his meals brought up. All the time he was growing bigger and stronger, Ben's mum grew thinner and more tired. Until one day, she said, "I'm quite worn out." Ben's dad sent her to bed and called the doctor who said, "You're to stay in bed a day or two and let someone look after you."

The grobblop heard what the doctor said. He peeped in to see Ben's mum. "She does look so sad and small," thought the grobblop who was now big and strong. He felt ashamed. He went downstairs at once.

He cleaned the kitchen, dusted the rooms, and made a delicious meal which he took up to her on a tray. He did this every day until Ben's mum was well again. Then he said to her, "I've come to say it's time I went away."

"You don't have to go," said Ben's mum. "You can really stay as long as you like."

But the grobblop replied, "No, I'm big enough and strong enough to look after myself now. I won't forget how well you looked after me and I'll write to you sometimes."

Ben and his mum and dad were quite sorry to say goodbye to the grobblop. He went to live at the seaside and he did write to them. He sent them some lovely picture postcards and he's asked them to come and stay with him for their next summer holiday.

These timid monsters are very shy and they do their very best to scare frightening children away!

THE MONSTER TREE

Terry Jones

There was once a tree that grew in a wood not far from here. It was a very special tree. Its leaves were red and its trunk was green and on it grew apples that were bright blue. And nobody ever ate the bright blue apples that hung from the tree, because they knew if they did they would meet a monster before the day was out.

One day a boy was walking with his mother in the wood, and they passed the Monster Tree. "Oh, can I have one of those bright blue apples?" said the boy.

"No," said his mother, "you know you mustn't, because anyone who eats one will meet a monster before the day is out."

The little boy didn't say anything, but he thought to himself: "Piffle!" and he resolved there and then that he would try one of those bright blue apples for himself.

So that night, when his mother and father were safely tucked up in bed, he took his satchel and stole out of the house and down the garden and through the village. The moon made everything blue and silver, and the houses looked dark and sinister, and he began to feel a little bit frightened at being all on his own.

Soon he came to the end of the village, and he looked along the lonely path that led to the wood where the Monster Tree grew, and he felt even more frightened. "But I don't believe in monsters," he said to himself, and he set off along the path.

Before long he came to the edge of a wood. The trees stretched up high above him, and the wood was dark and full of strange noises, and he didn't like it at all. But he said to himself: "I'm not scared of monsters." Then he summoned up all his courage and stepped into the dark wood.

Well, he hadn't gone far before he heard a hideous noise, and he saw a horrible pair of yellow eyes peering out at him from the darkness, and a terrible voice said: "You'll make a tasty meal for the monsters in the wood."

He was so frightened that his knees knocked together, but he kept on walking. And he hadn't gone much farther when there was an awful screech, and something flew out of a tree and pulled his hair and screamed: "The monsters are hungry tonight! The monsters are hungry tonight!"

Now he was so scared that his teeth started chattering, but he kept on walking towards the Monster Tree.

And just as he was passing an old hollow oak, a terrible creature leapt out in front of him, with great long nails and burning eyes and fire coming out of its ears, and it screamed: "They'll break your bones! They'll drink your blood! Go back!"

And the boy was so frightened that his hair stood on end, and he nearly turned right round and ran home to his bed. But he didn't. And the creature gave a terrible shriek and rushed at him.

The boy jumped up and grabbed a branch, and then leapt over the creature's head, and ran as fast as he could until he reached the Monster Tree. He pulled off as many of the bright blue apples as he could carry in his satchel, and ran home as fast as his legs could take him. And when he got home, he jumped into bed, hid under the blankets and ate one of the bright blue apples from the Monster Tree all alone in the dark, and then he fell asleep.

In his dreams that night he met more monsters than you could ever imagine in a whole year. And when he woke up the next morning, he told his mother all about the Monster Tree and his terrible journey in the night. His mother was very cross, and she took his satchel and opened it up to throw those apples from the Monster Tree on the fire. But when she looked into the satchel she couldn't see any bright blue apples - they were just ordinary apples. And that morning, the villagers went into the wood to cut the Monster Tree down, but do you know what? They couldn't find it. And to this day it has never been seen again.

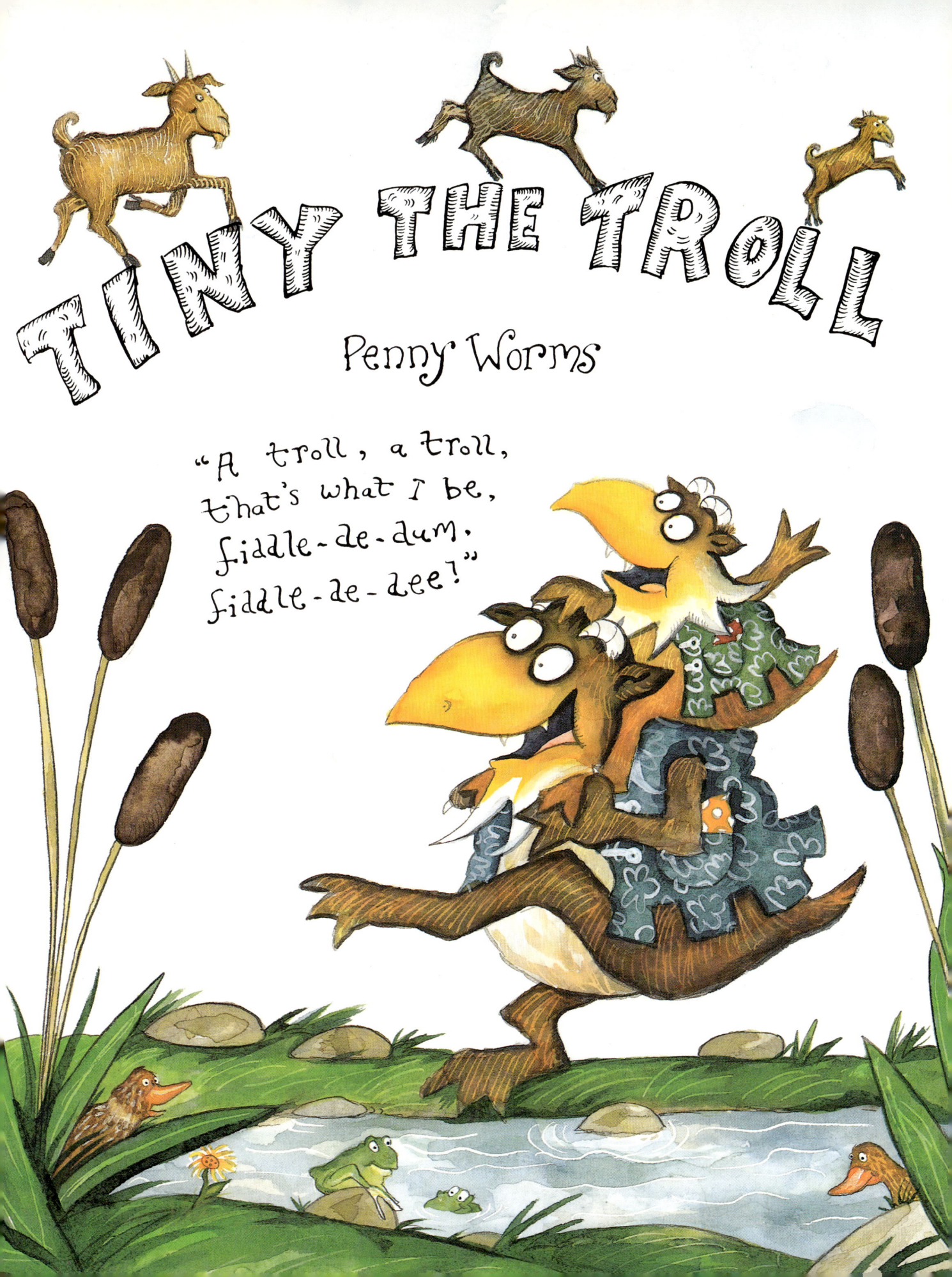

TINY THE TROLL

Penny Worms

"A troll, a troll, that's what I be, fiddle-de-dum, fiddle-de-dee!"

Tiny the Troll hated Wednesdays. It was the one day in the week when his parents gave him and his big brother lessons in how to be a proper troll. But Tiny didn't want to learn how to be mean and wicked. He didn't want to have to frighten people. And he didn't want to learn the silly troll song.

"You've got to grow up to be as mean as your ol' pa," said his father.

"You've got to study troll ways, sweetie," said his mother.

"Come on, Tiny," said his brother. "I'll help you learn. It's fun, really it is."

But Tiny knew what was going to happen. He knew that as soon as he learnt how to be a proper troll, he would have to leave his wonderful home and family. He would have to go to wherever the Chief Troll sent him. That is what all trolls must do. . . and that is exactly what happened.

The day came when Tiny had to go off into the big wide world and put all his troll training into practice. His brother had left months before and Tiny knew his time was drawing near.

"Son, the Chief Troll has given you a particularly special task," said his father. "He wants you to go and protect the bridge where the three Billy-Goats Gruff live. You must never, and I mean never, let them cross that rickety-rackety old bridge."

So off Tiny went to make his new home all alone on the swampy river bank, underneath the rickety-rackety old bridge.

He often peeked out to see those three Billy-Goats Gruff having fun, playing together in their field. It made him long for his own home and his own family.

"It's tough being a troll," he said to himself with a great sigh. Then one day all his troll training was put to the test. He couldn't believe his ears. Someone was crossing his bridge.

Trip, trap, trip, trap, went the noise. Trip, trap, trip, trap.

Tiny leapt out to see who it was and there standing in front of him was the smallest Billy-Goat Gruff. They eyed one another and Tiny knew what he had to do. In his loudest voice he said:

"A troll, a troll, that's what I be,
Fiddle-de-dum, fiddle-de-dee,
We're mean and mad and very, very bad,
And we eat billy-goats for our breakfast."

In fact, he wasn't the slightest bit hungry and the last thing he would have eaten was the little Billy-Goat Gruff, but the troll song was an important part of troll training.

"Oh, don't eat me," squealed the smallest Billy-Goat Gruff. "I just want to go across to the green, green meadow and eat the sweet grass there. Besides, my brother will be along in a minute and he'd make a bigger and better meal than me."

Tiny thought it was unfair of the little Billy-Goat Gruff's brother to let his little brother cross the bridge first. His own brother would never have let him do that. He decided to teach that big Billy-Goat Gruff a lesson and so he let the little Billy-Goat Gruff pass.

It wasn't long before he heard the big Billy-Goat Gruff on his bridge.

TRIP, TRAP, TRIP, TRAP, went the noise. TRIP, TRAP, TRIP, TRAP.

Up Tiny jumped and there standing before him was the big Billy-Goat Gruff. In his biggest, hugest, loudest voice, he sang:

"A troll, a troll, that's what I be,
Fiddle-de-dum, fiddle-de-dee,
We're mean and mad and very, very bad,
And we eat billy-goats for our breakfast."

The big Billy-Goat Gruff looked a little scared seeing Tiny, with his eyes as large as saucers and his long, pointed nose.

"Oh, don't eat me," cried the big Billy-Goat Gruff. "I only want to join my brother in the green, green meadow to eat the sweet grass there. Besides, my brother will be along in a minute and he'll make a bigger and better meal than me."

Although Tiny was angry with this Billy-Goat Gruff, he thought it even more unfair that the biggest Billy-Goat Gruff had let both his smaller brothers cross the bridge before him. His brother would never have done that. So he let the big Billy-Goat Gruff pass.

It wasn't long before he heard the biggest Billy-Goat Gruff on his bridge.

TRIP, TRAP, TRIP, TRAP, went the noise. TRIP, TRAP, TRIP, TRAP.

Up Tiny jumped and there before him stood the biggest Billy-Goat Gruff. In his realiest, truliest, loudest voice, he shouted:

"A troll, a troll, that's what I be,
Fiddle-de-dum, fiddle-de-dee,
We're mean and mad and very, very bad,
And we eat billy-goats for our breakfast."

The biggest Billy-Goat Gruff didn't look the slightest bit scared.

"Ha, ha," he cried. "I have no fears.

On my head I've two sharp spears.

On my feet I've four hard stones.

I'll knock you out and break your bones."

And with that, the biggest Billy-Goat Gruff charged at Tiny and knocked him clean off the bridge and went TRIP, TRAP, TRIP, TRAPPING across the bridge to the green, green meadow to eat the sweet grass with his brothers.

Luckily that was not the end of Tiny the Troll. The river carried him far, far away from the rickety-rackety old bridge. Far, far away from the green, green meadow. Far, far away from those Billy-Goats Gruff.

When the river washed Tiny ashore, he had no idea where he was. He wiped his eyes as big as saucers and blew his long, pointed nose and looked around. That's when he heard it. That's when he heard the silly, wonderful troll song.

"A troll, a troll, that's what I be,
Fiddle-de-dum, fiddle-de-dee,
We're mean and mad and very, very bad,
And we eat billy-goats for our breakfast."

There standing in front of him, smiling broadly, was his very own brother.

And that is where you can find them to this day. Sitting under a wibbly-wobbly bridge singing that silly troll song.

I was building sand castles on the beach when this charming dragon offered to help. He had a lovely bucket and spade that Irma had given him.

IRRITATING IRMA

Robin Klein

Irma was very good at climbing. Her parents were calm people, who, if they saw Irma clamber up a church steeple or the outside of a lighthouse, would just murmur admiringly, "Lovely, darling." So when they took a holiday cottage near some steep cliffs and Irma told them she was going looking for eagles, they just said, "Lovely, darling."

Irma began to climb the cliffs and half-way up she found a little door. The door belonged to a dragon who was having a very nice long sleep, and he wasn't a bit pleased to be woken up. He stared at Irma's teeth, braces and glasses and he wasn't very impressed. He rumbled like a forge.

"What a cute green lizard!" said Irma.

The dragon, insulted, uttered a huge echoey roar, which splintered granite flakes from his cave.

"That's a nasty cough you've got," said Irma.

The dragon eyed her Spiderman T-shirt and torn jeans and the cap that she had got free from a service station. He remembered clearly that maidens usually wore dear little gold crowns and embroidered slippers, and they always squealed when they met him and looked ill at ease. He glared at Irma and spurted forth a long, smoky orange flame.

"No wonder you've got a cough," Irma said. "Smoking's a nasty habit and bad for your health. And this cave certainly is musty. It needs airing."

The dragon made a noise like bacon rashers frying, but Irma was busy inspecting everything. "You need a broom for a start," she said. "And maybe a cuckoo clock up there by the door. Tch! Just look at the dust over everything! Tomorrow I'll bring some cleaning equipment and anything else I can think of."

When she left, the dragon set to work, only he didn't do any dusting. He collected boulders and filled up the cave entrance. Bouldered up, and fortressed up, and buttressed up, he smiled grimly to himself and went back to sleep.

Some hours later he woke to a whirring, headachey rumbling. Granite chips rattled around his ears, and Irma scrambled in, carrying a bright pneumatic power drill.

"Good morning," she called. "There must have been a landslide during the night. But I cleaned it up."

The dragon's scales rattled. Angry little flames flickered in his jaw. He made a noise like a hundred barbecues and he squinted ferociously at Irma.

"Don't frown like that," she ordered, tying on an apron. "You'll end up with ugly worry lines. There's a lot of work to get through this morning. First I'll sweep this gritty sand away, and you could really do with a nice carpet in here, or maybe tiles would be better. If there's one thing I just can't stand, it's disorder."

The dragon sizzled fretfully, but worse was to come. When Irma finished tidying up, she turned her attention to him. She bossily trimmed and lacquered his claws. She polished his scales and lifted up his wings and dusted under them with talcum powder. The dragon blushed but Irma didn't take any notice, because she was busy tying a blue ribbon around his tail. "I've got to be going now," she said. "But I'll be back tomorrow."

The dragon watched her climb down the cliff. "There's only one way to get any peace," he thought. "I'll just have to eat her. Freckles will taste nasty, and so will ginger hair, but maybe if I shut my eyes and gulp, it won't be so bad." He groaned. Parents, he knew from past experience, usually came looking for devoured maidens, waving lances and acting very unfriendly.

When Irma arrived the next morning, he opened his jaws, without much enthusiasm, ready to eat her, but Irma said, "Look what I brought you!"

She shoved a plate under his nose. On it was a layer cake with strawberry cream filling, iced with chocolate icing, sprinkled with hundreds and thousands, lollies, whipped cream and meringues. The dragon shuddered weakly and felt ill.

"You look as though you're coming down with the flu," said Irma. She took his temperature and spread a blanket over him. The blanket was fluffily pink and edged with satin binding, and the dragon thought it was very babyish. Irma wrapped it around him and fastened it with a kitten brooch. "I'll leave you to get some rest now, you poor old thing," she said.

"You will?" thought the dragon hopefully.

"But I'll drop by first thing tomorrow," said Irma. "It's lucky for you I still have three weeks of my holiday left."

And for three weeks, every day, she came, and the dragon suffered. She decorated his cave with pot plants and cushions, a beanbag chair, posters, a book case, calendars, and a dart board, and she brought along a toothbrush and bullied him into cleaning his teeth.

But at last, one morning she said, "I've got to go back to school tomorrow. You'll have to look after yourself till next summer holidays."

When Irma left, the dragon purred and capered about the cave. "Hooray!" he thought. "Good riddance! No more boring chatter and no more being organised, and best of all, undisturbed sleep!" He curled up and shut his eyes.

But his dreams were fretful, and he got up at daybreak feeling tetchy and cross. He paced his cave and wondered why the silence seemed so weary, and the hours bleak and long. He brooded and nibbled at a claw, and crouched in his doorway staring down at the beach, but it was empty, because all the holiday people had gone. Irma had gone.

"Hooray!" he roared. "And she won't be back for many glorious months!"

But why, he wondered glumly, were tears rolling down his cheeks?

Everywhere he looked in his cave he saw things Irma had lugged up the cliff to decorate his cave without permission.

"Yuk," said the dragon morosely, and he kicked a pot plant over the cliff. A wave snatched at it, and the dragon gave a roar of anger and slithered down the cliff to grab it back. He carried it crossly back to his cave and plonked it down on Irma's bookcase.

"Even when she's not here, she's irritating," he thought. "I should have eaten her and got it over with. The very next time I see her, irritating Irma will be my next meal! Freckles and all! Just wait!"

And he waited, but all his little flames flickered out one by one, and his scales lost their sparkle, and his ribboned tail drooped listlessly. Winter howled through his cave, and he brooded, and led a horrid bad-tempered life.

But at last gay umbrellas began to blossom like flowers along the beach, and it was summer. The dragon sharpened his teeth against the rocks and tried to work up an appetite. And the day came when Irma bounced in through his door, and the indignant dragon opened his jaws wide.

"Hello!" cried Irma. "I meant to write, but I forgot your address, but just look what I brought you! Suntan lotion, and a yo-yo with a long string so it will reach down to the bottom of the cliff, and a kite with a picture of you on it, and now tell me did you miss me? I certainly missed you!"

The dragon blinked in despair at her tangly plaits and glasses and teeth braces. "She's talkative and tedious and her manners are terrible!" he reminded himself fiercely.

("And yet," he thought, "it's strange, but I rather like her face.")

"Nonsense!" he roared to himself. "She's annoying and bossy and an utter little nuisance, and no one invited her here; she just walks in as though she owns this whole cliff!"

("And yet," he thought, "of all the maidens all forlorn, I rather like her the best.")

"Didn't you miss me?" demanded Irma.

The dragon began to shake his head indignantly, but try as he could to prevent it, the headshake turned into a nod.

"Then we'll celebrate," said Irma. "What would you like for lunch?"

"Plain scones, please, Irma," said the dragon.

This friendly monster would love to have some visitors. He bakes fresh biscuits every Thursday, so pop in and say "Hello!"

FRIGHTENING THE MONSTER IN WIZARD'S HOLE

Grrr Grrr!

Margaret Mahy

One day a truckload of bricks went over a bump and two bricks fell off into the middle of the road. They lay there like two newly laid oblong eggs, dropped by some unusual bird. A boy called Tom-Tom, coming down the road, stopped to look at them. He picked one up. It was a beautiful glowing orange-coloured brick and it seemed as if it should be used for something special, but what can you do that's special with only one brick, or even two?

"Hey, Tom-Tom!" called his friend Sam Bucket coming up behind him. "What are you doing with that brick?"

"Just holding it," Tom-Tom said, "holding it and thinking. . ."

"Thinking what?"

". . . thinking that I'd take it and throw it really hard at. . ."

"At whom, Tom-Tom?"

"At the monster in Wizard's Hole."

Sam's eyes and mouth opened like early morning windows. "You'd be too scared."

"No, I wouldn't. That's what I'm going to do now."

Tom-Tom set off down the road with his bright orange brick. Sam Bucket did not see why Tom-Tom should have all the glory and adventure. He grabbed the brick that was left in the middle of the road.

"Hang on, Tom-Tom! I'm coming too."

"Okay!" said Tom-Tom grandly. "But don't forget it's my idea, so I'm going to throw first."

"Where are you two off to?" asked a farmer, leaning over his gate.

"We're going to throw these bricks at the monster in Wizard's Hole," explained Tom-Tom.

"He's going to throw first and I'm going to throw next," cried Sam boastfully.

"You'd never dare!" cried the farmer.

"We're on our way now," they said together, strutting like bantam roosters along the sunny, dusty road.

"But how are you going to get the monster out of Wizard's Hole?" asked the farmer. "He hasn't looked out for years."

"I shall shout at him," declared Tom grandly. "I shall say, 'Come on, Monster, out you come!' and he'll have to come, my voice will be so commanding."

"I shall shout too," said Sam Bucket quickly. " I shall say, 'Come out, Monster. Come out and have bricks thrown at you.' My voice will be like a lion's roar. He'll have to come."

Off went Tom-Tom, Sam Bucket and the farmer, all holding bricks, all marching with a sense of purpose. They passed Mrs Puddenytame's Pumpkin Farm. Mrs Puddenytame herself was out, subduing the wild twining pumpkins.

"You lot look pleased with yourselves," she remarked as they passed by.

"We are," said Tom-Tom, "because we're on our way to do great things. You see these bricks? We're on our way to throw them at the monster in Wizard's Hole."

"You'd never dare!" breathed Mrs Puddenytame. "Why, they say that the monster is all lumpy and bumpy, horrible, hairy and hideous – and besides, he hasn't bothered anyone for over a hundred years."

"He's there, isn't he?" asked Sam Bucket. "Come out, we'll say, out you come, Monster, and have bricks thrown at you."

"He'll have to come," cried the farmer. "And when he feels our bricks he'll run like a rabbit. We'll be heroes to the whole country."

"Well, hang on then!" Mrs Puddenytame shouted. "I've got a few spare bricks myself – and seven sons too." And she hunted the sons out of the pumpkins shouting, "Come on, you louts! You can be heroes too."

"But, Mother," said her eldest, cleverest son, "nobody else wants Wizard's Hole. Why shouldn't the monster stay there?"

"He's a monster, isn't he?" yelled Mrs Puddenytame. "Who ever heard of rights for monsters. You get a brick and come along with the rest of us." Off they went, eleven people all carrying bricks down the sunny, dusty road to town.

Once they got to town, people came out of their houses to watch them. People followed them down the road. There was quite a procession by the time they reached the town square with the fountain in the middle of it. There Tom-Tom made a speech.

"Friends," he cried, "the time has come to act. We are going to throw bricks at the monster in Wizard's Hole."

"We're going to roar like lions," added Sam Bucket.

"And stamp like bulls!" agreed the farmer stamping.

"We're going to laugh like hyenas, and shriek like mad parrots," Mrs Puddenytame shouted, "and frighten the monster into the next country. We've had the monster for too long. Let someone else have him."

"Hooray!" shouted all the people.

"The monster will run..." promised Tom-Tom.

"He'll flee!" agreed Sam Bucket.

"He'll fly!" gloated the farmer.

"He'll bound and pound and turn head over heels!" declared Mrs Puddenytame, weighing her brick in her hand.

"I think I'll get a brick too," said the Mayor thoughtfully, looking at a truckload of bricks parked by a building construction site. "Nothing should be done without a Mayor."

"Don't forget the schoolchildren!" cried an anxious teacher. "Remember they are the citizens of tomorrow."

"But what are we doing it for?" asked a small child, surprised.

"For the good of the community. Go and find a brick," commanded the teacher.

Soon everyone had taken a brick from the back of the truck and was marching sternly towards Wizard's Hole.

The monster was just sitting down to a breakfast of fried eggs and crisp bacon when he heard the sound of many feet marching towards his front door.

"Visitors – at last!" thought the monster. He rushed to his bed cave, put on a collar and tie, washed behind his ears and brushed his many teeth. Then he ran to his front door and put his head out of Wizard's Hole.

"Good morning!" he said and smiled. Everyone stopped. Tom-Tom stopped, Sam Bucket stopped. The farmer, Mrs Puddenytame and her seven sons, the Mayor and the school teacher – everyone stopped.

"Come on in. . . I'm just making fresh coffee." The monster smiled again showing his newly brushed teeth. He had a lot of teeth, this monster, all of them sharp. Everyone stared.

"Do come in. I'm so pleased to see you," wheedled the monster. But the monster was wheedling in monster language which is a mixture of growling, whining, roaring and shrieking. Every single person dropped his brick. Every single solitary person ran without looking back once.

"Goodness me!" said the monster looking at the bricks. "Are all these presents for me? Too kind! Too kind! Thank you. . ." he called after them. But he said the thank you in monster language which is a mixture of rumbling, snarling and screaming.

Everyone ran even faster than before.

The monster went in and put on his bricklayer's apron, got his bricklayer's trowel and made himself a handsome brick monster house. Then he moved out of Wizard's Hole which had always been so damp that the wallpaper peeled off, and he lived happily ever after.

And when Tom-Tom heard what had happened he said: "Well, we got him out of Wizard's Hole anyway."

And felt very successful.

Watch out for these naughty monsters!

Ten hungry monsters

Susan Heyboer O'Keefe

One hungry monster underneath my bed,
moaning and groaning and begging to be fed.

Two hungry monsters at my wardrobe door,
chewing up my trainers, asking me for more.

Three hungry monsters in the upstairs hall,
lick the flower painting hanging on the wall.

Four hungry monsters round my Daddy's head,
sniffing out the crackers he'd eaten in his bed.

Five hungry monsters sliding down the rail,
munching and crunching on one another's tail.

Six hungry monsters underneath the rug,
tracking down some footprints to catch a tasty bug.

Seven hungry monsters round our TV screen,
drooling at commercials for sauerkraut and beans.

Eight hungry monsters on the chandeliers,
swear they haven't eaten for maybe twenty years.

Nine hungry monsters wearing roller skates,
hunting through the kitchen for knives and forks and plates.

Ten hungry monsters, about to fuss and kick,
won't get out, they tell me, unless I feed them quick!

So I bring out one jug of apple juice,
two loaves of bread,
three bowls of spaghetti that they dump upon my head,
four purple eggplants,
five pickled pears,
six orange pumpkins they climb up and down like stairs,
seven roasted turkeys,
eight pizza pies,
nine watermelons that they wish were twice the size,
ten jars of peanut butter, but not a speck of jam
(because I want every monster mouth shut tighter than a clam).

They gargle with some apple juice, then shower with the rest.
They pinch the bread to bread crumbs and won't clean up their mess.
They braid spaghetti into wigs and eat the eggplants whole,
and learn that pickled pears won't bounce – and neither will they roll.

They wear the pumpkin tops as hats and dream of pumpkin pie.
They argue over wishbones and pick the turkeys dry.
They toss the pizzas back and forth like Frisbees throught the air,
then spit out sticky melon seeds to land right in my hair.

They paint the peanut butter like lipstick on their mouths,
then stamp their feet and boldly say, "What ELSE is in
this house?"

"Get out, get out!"
I loudly shout.
"You've made a mess
and then, no less,
you ate my food,
and were quite rude.
You put me in a nasty mood.
You are so bad
it makes me mad!
It makes me want
to squirm and twist,
to make a face,
and shake my fist,
to stamp the floor
and kick the door;
and then to do it
all once more!
And so without
a single doubt,
I tell you now —
get out, get out!"

Ten sorry monsters, creeping one by one,
climb into the chimney, and now my job is done.

Then from behind the toaster, my secret hiding spot,
I take an apple pie the monsters never got!

The compiler and publisher wish to thank all the authors, agents and publishers and other copyright holders who kindly granted us permission to use the stories in this anthology.
"Granny Monster's Bedtime Story" by Andrew Matthews from *Monster Hullabaloo* published by Methuen Children's Books, reproduced by permission of Reed Consumer Books Ltd. "The Dragon of an Ordinary Family" by Margaret Mahy, illustrated by Helen Oxenbury, published by William Heinemann Ltd, reproduced by permission of Reed Consumer Books Ltd. "The Hairy Monster" by Henriette Bichonnier, translated by Adrian Sington from the original publication by Gallimard, reproduced by permission of Moonlight Publishing Ltd. "The Green Grobblop" by Eugenie Summerfield from *Animal Tales from Listen With Mother* published by Hutchinson, reproduced by permission of the author. "The Monster Tree" by Terry Jones from *Fairy Tales* published by Pavilion, reproduced by permission of Pavilion. "Tiny the Troll" by Penny Worms, copyright © Penny Worms 1995. "Irritating Irma" by Robin Klein from *Ratbags and Rascals*, published by Victor Gollancz, copyright © Robin Klein 1980 reproduced by permission of Curtis Brown, London. "Frightening the Monster in Wizard's Hole" by Margaret Mahy from *Nonstop Nonsense* published by J M Dent & Sons Ltd, reproduced by permission of J M Dent & Sons Ltd. "Ten Hungry Monsters" by Susan Heyboer O'Keefe from *One Hungry Monster* published by Joy Street Books, copyright © 1989 Susan Heyboer O'Keefe, reproduced by permission of Little, Brown and Company. Every effort has been made to trace all the copyright holders and the publishers apologise if any inadvertent omission has been made.
Copyright this edition © Orchard Books 1995

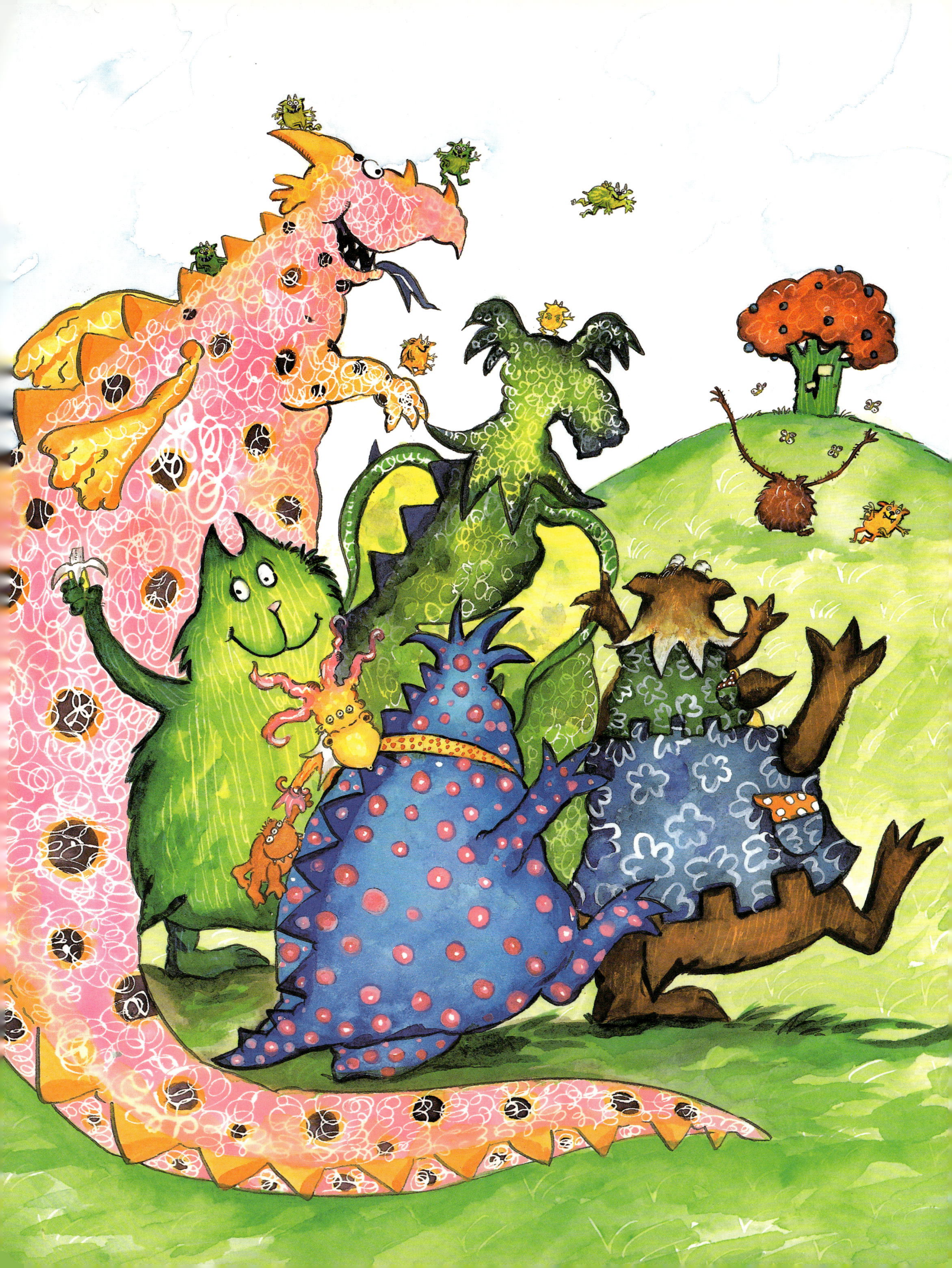

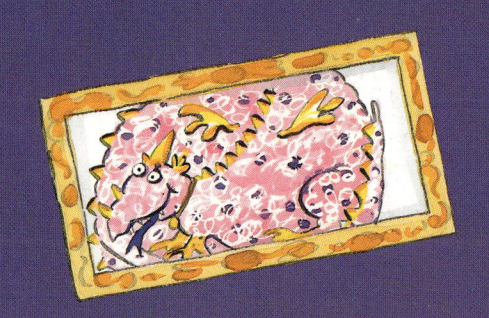

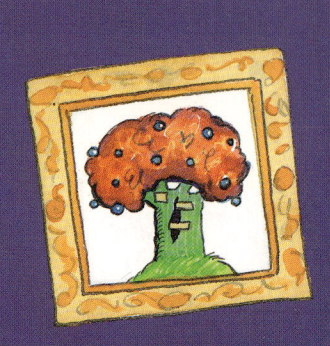